Acknowledgements

I would like to thank my daughter Halle and my wife and "best friend" Belinda for editing this book. Thanks to my daughter Savannah and son Micah for allowing me to be their Sunday School Teacher. Finally, I would like to thank our Children's Pastor, Kathy Powell for allowing us to serve and share the love of Jesus Christ to students for almost 14 years. With God, all things are possible!

Foreword

After spending several years teaching pre-teens the Word of God, I have always found it a challenge to keep kids interested and the lessons applicable. As a homeschooling parent, my wife and I have taught science lessons with our three children. We decided to do this at our place of worship and have found this to be a great success with our Sunday school class. I have even used some experiments on a mission trip in Central America with great success. The Lord has placed it upon my heart to develop a "21st century parable" manual to help teachers incorporate science projects with a Bible study for their respective classes.

Many of us can probably remember lessons in Sunday School where we felt "lectured" to in our respective classes. It is amazing how we can take some ordinary household items and allow the Lord to speak through them. There is a movement within the church to make Sunday School classes more interactive and exciting with more activities. While I don't agree with all of the changes, I do think God's Word is exciting and can be delivered in an exciting manner. I pray that this will be a blessing to you and your students.

Note: all Scriptures listed are taken from the New International Version (NIV) unless otherwise indicated.

ISBN-13:978-1732602205
ISBN-10:1732602204
Copyright © Reginald D. Bullard
Published by A Blessed Heritage Educational Resources. Further reproduction by any means, electronic or mechanical, including photocopying and recording, or by any information storage or retrieval system, must be arranged with the copyright holder noted.

Chapter 1
What Can Jesus Do For You?

Key Background Scriptures:

Matthew 4:18-22

Matthew 17:1-5

Matthew 16:13-19

Matthew 14:22-33

Matthew 26:69-75

Caution
I recommend wearing safety goggles for this experiment. Also note that the nail will get pretty hot. I suggest using an oven mitt to handle the battery.

This title comes from a commercial for the United Parcel Service (UPS™) that became popular in the early 2000's. The company's slogan was "What can Brown do for you?"

Summary
The learning objective is for students to understand the importance of being connected with Christ. The experiment uses battery currents to show the value of the right connections and what happens when we do not connect with Jesus Christ. The Spiritual lesson is that when we connect with Christ, all former habits (behaviors, etc.) will no longer seem important.

THE LESSON:

Say to students:
We need to understand that we do not love Jesus for what He can do; we love Him for who He is. Yet, we owe it to ourselves to recognize that because we are in Christ, we are different. The Bible says that "If any man be in Christ, He is a new creature. Old things are passed away; all things are become new..." 2nd Corinthians 5:17. If we get a true revelation of who we are, some of the things we find fascinating will not interest us

anymore. Some of the behaviors we think are cute, or some of the friends we think are cool, just will not be the same anymore.

As we talk about Peter, I want you to think about whether anything you do shows others that you are a Christian. What makes you different from anyone else at your school, saved, or unsaved? Is your own life ordinary, or is it extraordinary? If being a Christian was a crime, would be there enough evidence to convict you?

Ask: Who was Peter?
(Possible correct answers include):

The leader of the 12 disciples (Matthew 17:1-5)

A man that was willing to be used by God (Matthew 14:22-33)

Say to students: **One of the first voices of the Gospel and in the book of Acts- (Matthew 16:13-19)**
Peter acknowledged that Jesus was not only a prophet, but He was the Son of the Living God! Jesus agreed with Peter and confirmed the power that Peter would have here on earth. Peter, James and John were the closest disciples to Jesus.

Peter was close to Jesus, like a best friend. Discuss some of the differences between friends and best friends.

Activity: Have students develop a table similar to the one below:

Friends	Best Friends

Other key points to discuss:

Peter was the first disciple willing to take a risk and walk on the water towards Jesus, BUT, Peter also took his eyes off of Jesus and began to sink. Jesus wants us to develop a close relationship with Him, but we will sink if he we take our eyes off of Him throughout our lives.

Peter was an ordinary man with ordinary fears- (Matthew 26:69-75)

After Jesus was arrested, Peter denied Jesus three times and began to weep bitterly because of his actions. If you look at verses 33-35 in Matthew 26, Peter vowed to be with Jesus until the end. Unfortunately, Peter could not handle the pressure from the crowd. How many times have we pledged our love and devotion to Jesus, but found it not cool to follow Him when we get pressure from the crowd? We want to fit in and do not want criticism for our Christian walk sometimes.

Peter did mighty things for Christ, but he was indeed an ordinary man with ordinary fears.

Science Experiment

Supplies

- (Any size cell{AA, A, C or D}) Do not use a battery of higher voltage than a D battery. *The battery-represents God.*
- 2 feet of insulated wire. Strip both ends of the wire so that the bare conductor is exposed. (Do not use wire that is thicker than 18 gauge)- *The wire represents our relationship with God.*
- Large iron nail (at least 3 inches long)-*The nail represents us.*
- Electrical Tape- *The tape represents how we connect with Christ.*
- Metal Paper Clip-*This represents the things that we attract (favor, anointing, spiritual gifts, things that only God can provide)*
- Eye protection such as goggles or safety glasses
- Oven Mitt

Experiment Steps

1. Show the nail to the class. **Say to students…**Peter was nothing but a fisherman. God can use ordinary people like us to do great things for Him.
2. Lay the paper clip out on a table or desk.
3. Take the nail and touch the paper clip.
4. Pull the nail away and show that the paper clip would not attach to the nail. **Say to students…** Peter found that, on his own he could not attract anything, not even fish.
5. Make sure that the wire is stripped at the end so that the bare conductor is exposed.
6. Wrap the wire around the nail as many times as you can. The tighter you can wrap the wire around the nail, the more turns of wire you have for the students, the better. **Say to students…** What is it that you want in a relationship? You want to hold on to God and don't let go. God only has this level of intimacy for certain types of relationships. The battery represents our powerful God. Peter was willing to get connected with God.
7. Show the electrical tape and describe the bonding power **Ask students…** What connects you? (Possible answers include Bible study, participating in Sunday School, praying, witnessing, etc.).
8. Use the tape to attach the bare conductor on one end of the wire to the top of the battery and the other bare conductor to the other end of the battery. Electricity will flow through the wire very quickly. With the electricity still flowing, touch the nail to the paper clip. The paper clip should attach itself to the nail. **Say to students.** When Peter connected with God, he was on fire for God. He became a leader of the disciples, an early leader of the Christian church, a writer and one of the three men to be with Jesus on the mountain.

Chapter 2
Being Filled with the Holy Spirit

One summer, our youth pastor decided to use the theme of "Power Lab" for Vacation Bible School. All of the classrooms and our large Family Life Center were decorated and designed as a scientific lab. We decided to conduct a simple experiment that discussed the power of the Holy Spirit.

Summary

The learning objective of the lesson is for students to learn the characteristics of being filled with the Holy Spirit. *I would suggest that you conduct this experiment outside.* The cola will literally go up to 20 feet in the air. You probably do not want this to hit the ceiling and then fall to the floor in your church! Also, I recommend buying certain gadgets for this, but you can certainly buy most of the items at a grocery store. Just keep in mind that you might get a "cola shower" if you cannot run away in time. The Spiritual Lesson is to identify the various attributes of the Fruit of the Spirit.

Key Background Scriptures

Galatians 5:19—23

John 14:16-17

John 14:25

Acts 2:4

THE LESSON:

Say to students…

There are behavioral differences between those who are filled with the Fruit of the Spirit and the Holy Spirit and those who are not.

Given a poor choice of everyday examples, a student might ask, how does a Christian behave? In John 14:16-17, Jesus promises the Holy Spirit for all believers. As Jesus was preparing to leave the disciples, He sent the Holy Spirit to provide counsel and wisdom for us. In addition, the Holy Spirit will live in us as well. (John 14:25)

Ask: What are the characteristics of those who are not filled with the Holy Spirit?

Tell the students to read:
Galatians 5:19-23

- Sexual immorality
- Impurity and debauchery
- Idolatry and witchcraft
- Hatred
- Discord
- Jealously
- Fits of rage
- Selfish ambition
- Dissensions
- Factions and envy
- Drunkenness and orgies

Say to students... Unfortunately, those who live with the above characteristics will not inherit the kingdom of God. Christians can struggle with any of these, but we should seek healing and deliverance through prayer.

What are the characteristics of those who are filled with the Holy Spirit?

- Love
- Joy
- Peace
- Patience
- Kindness
- Goodness
- Faithfulness
- Gentleness
- Self-Control

Science Experiment

Steve Spangler has a wonderful guide for conducting the diet cola experiment. You can gather more information by going to www.stevespanglerscience.com .

Supplies

- 10 2 Liter Bottles of diet cola
- 10 rolls or boxes of Mentos Mints®
- Geyser tube and pin (can be ordered from www.stevespangerscience.com)
- Index Cards

Directions

1. Take 10 2-Liter bottles of diet cola and use index cards to put the following labels on them: (Holy Spirit, Wisdom, Kindness, Peace, Love, Joy, Patience, Goodness, Faithfulness, Gentleness and Self-Control)

2. Take the top off the bottle of 2 Liter diet cola and attach the geyser tube with the pin inserted into the hole.

3. **Say to students**: Discuss the effects of being filled with the Holy Spirit and attach the geyser tube at the top of each bottle. Add 7 Mentos® tabs to each 2 liter bottle of diet cola.

4. When you pull the pin, the 7 Mentos® tabs will drop into the bottle and you will have a geyser that will go approximately 20 feet into the air.

5. **Say to students**: When the geyser is coming forth, you can discuss that we are now overflowing with Wisdom.

Since kids will probably ask you can do this again, you can repeat the same process and discuss the other Fruits of the Spirit. The end results will yield an overflowing of Love, Joy, Patience, Goodness, etc. Just use a bottle of diet cola for each end result and you can convey the message.

Chapter 3
The Separation Principle

Summary

This lesson is great for pre-teens who are trying to live a Christ-filled life, but they are also balancing the negative peer-pressure in their environment. We discussed with our class the "separation principle". This lesson can be conducted inside and it allows others to safely participate in the experiment. This lesson does not require a lot of cleaning up and parents were very amazed to see the experiment in action.

Key Background Scriptures

Matthew 4:1-11
James 4:7

Say to students...

When we accept Jesus Christ as our Lord and Savior, we are washed clean and start a new life. However, we might still have the same temptations and pressures around us. The good news is that we can actually separate from those things and those things will separate from us. In James 4:7, the Bible says to "resist the devil and he will flee from you." The things that we did in the past will not mean the same to us and some of those old friends will notice a change in us, as well. In Matthew 4, Jesus was tempted in the desert by the devil. The devil used several different ways to tempt Jesus:

- **Tempted Him physically** - Satan knew that Jesus was hungry, so he challenged Jesus to eat (Matt 4:3)

- **Satan questioned God's protection during difficult situations**. He challenged Jesus to take a chance (Matt 4:6)

- **Satan tempted Jesus with possessions and power** (Matt 4:9) Satan told Jesus that if He would worship Satan, then he would give them to Him.

Science Experiment

<u>Supplies</u>

- Large Bowl
- Water

- Black Pepper
- Tweezers
- 1 1/2 inch chunk of soap taken from a soap bar

<u>Directions</u>

1. Fill the bowl ¾ full of water.

2. Shake pepper on the surface of the water. Make sure that the surface of the water is coated evenly with pepper.

3. Use tweezers to hold the chunk of soap and place it in the water covered with black pepper.

If you notice, the black pepper will actually move away from the soap. ***Say to students***: when we are washed and cleaned by Jesus' blood, then we are as clean as soap. Pressures and people will separate from us and we can separate from them (i.e., cheating at school, lying, being disobedient to our parents, etc.).

As discussed earlier, Jesus put this into practice in the book of Matthew. The devil left Jesus' presence because Jesus spoke the Word back to the devil. (Matthew 4:1-11) When we speak the Word back to our situation, those attitudes and behaviors have to flee. If you move the soap around with your tweezers, you will notice that the pepper will continue to move away. Discuss that we can put this into practice as we speak God's Word daily to ourselves and our situations.

Chapter Four
Keep your Light on for Him

(This lesson is actually a part 2 of the chapter 3 lesson of the Separation Principle). I had the opportunity to teach this lesson in the country of Belize to a Vacation Bible School class and also at a church service one Sunday. The response from the adults, as well as the children, was very positive.

Summary

This lesson is a great tool that can be used with adults as well as children. The response from one pastor in Belize was that this lesson was simple, but very powerful for everyone. All of the items can be easily found at your local grocery store. Small candles found at a dollar store are fine for this experiment.

Key Background Scriptures

Matthew 5:16

Matthew 13:1-23

Galatians 5:22-23

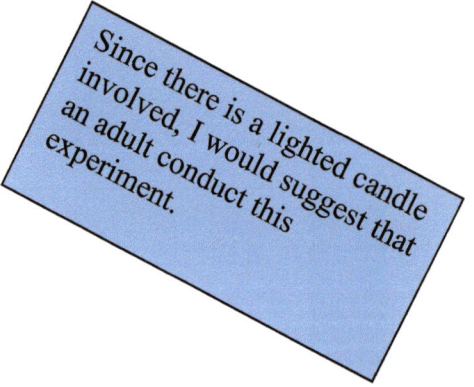

Since there is a lighted candle involved, I would suggest that an adult conduct this experiment.

Tell Students

Once we have made the decision to follow Jesus, we are expected to let our light shine for Him. (Matthew 5:16) There is no question that our light can shine in the midst of darkness and despair when we allow it to shine. The problem is that there are certain things that can snuff this light out or take it away.

THE LESSON

Ask Students… What snuffs out your light? (Give one of the examples below, and then allow them to respond).

- Not reading your Bible daily
- Lying

- Cheating
- Being disobedient to your parents/those in authority
- Not speaking God's promises over our lives and situations
- Allowing the things that we see to change our view as to how God sees situations

Parable of the Sower

There are some other ways where situations or people can also snuff out your light. Matthew 13:1-23 gives us the answer. Jesus shows when the worries of this life surround us, we will quickly lose faith in Him. Our light will literally be choked out because of the deceitfulness of wealth as well. Also, Satan can easily snatch the good Word inside of us if we are not careful. We will leave church excited one minute, but will easily become discouraged or negative the next minute. If we sow the seed into good fertile ground, then the crop will grow a hundredfold.

Ask Students... How does this happen?

- Focusing on what we see versus what God says through His promises
- Not having faith in Him
- Allowing negative people to affect our beliefs about God
- Following through on temptations
- Negative peer pressure from our friends at school, in the neighborhood, etc.
- Limited time with God; it is so easy to spend a brief time with God, but we can also easily return to our old ways as well

Science Experiment

Supplies

- A deep bowl so the candle will be below the sides of the bowl
- Small candle (a small tea light candle in a cup holder is suggested)
- A glass that will cover the candle
- One cup of vinegar
- One tablespoon of baking soda
- Matches or a lighter

Directions

1. Place the candle in the center of the bowl and light it.

2. *Say to students*… Review the characteristics of our light shining with the examples discussed in the Bible story. Some of the examples include trusting in God at all times, not following through with temptations, protecting your eyes/ears from negative things and using wisdom when following others' advice.

3. With the candle lit, take the glass and cover the candle. Notice that the light will extinguish. ***Say to students*…** Discuss the fact that when we don't read our Bible daily and we don't show the characteristics of the fruit of the spirit (Galatians 5:22) , then our light will immediately disappear.

4. Light the candle again and then slowly pour some vinegar around the candle in the bowl. ***Say to students*…** Discuss that vinegar represents the negative things/attitudes that surround us. (***They Stink*!!!**) Despite the things around us, our light can still shine and we are not affected by those things.

5. Keep the candle lit, but slowly add baking soda into the vinegar. **NOTE:** A chemical reaction occurs and eventually the baking soda and vinegar will yield carbon dioxide. In order for a flame to burn, it will need oxygen, not carbon dioxide. The carbon dioxide will fill the area around the flame. This pushes the oxygen out and the only thing left is the result of the vinegar and baking soda.

In our lives, we can survive with the vinegar (negative attitudes around us). However when we allow those negative attitudes to take over our lives and our thoughts, our light will eventually burn out. Again, don't let your light burn out!

Chapter 5
Don't Blend In

Summary

This experiment is very simple and kid-friendly. The lesson focuses on the importance of not conforming any longer to the pattern of this world, but being transformed by the renewing of your mind.

Key Background Scriptures

Romans 12:2
Daniel 1: 6-21
1st Cor. 12:14-26

Ask Students:

What does *transform* mean? What does *conform* mean?

This chapter discusses what happens when we stand for Christ and what happens when we do not stand for Christ. Many times pre-teens and teenagers succumb to negative peer pressure in schools, their neighborhoods and sometimes in their own churches. This is a short experiment that uses basic chemistry, but also discusses the importance of standing out for Jesus. This can also coincide with the lesson of Daniel, Shadrach, Meshach and Abednego (Daniel 1: 6-21).

In the book of Daniel, we see that it would have been easy for the four Israelites to simply follow the customs of the Babylonians and blend in. Here are some take-away points:

Say to students:
- **When you conform to the world, the world will sometimes give you a new name.**
- **When you don't conform to this world, God will still liberally supply all of your needs.**

As Christians, it is so easy to be like the rest of the world in a variety of situations, but we are called not to blend in.

Experiment 5

Supplies

- Five glasses
- Two stirring spoons
- Paper towel
- Measuring spoon that measures ½ teaspoon
- Sugar
- Table Salt
- Canola oil
- Olive oil

Directions

1. Fill four of the five glasses ¾ full with warm water
2. Measure out ½ teaspoon of sugar and mix it with the water in the first glass.
3. Use the same stirring spoon and try to dissolve ½ teaspoon of canola oil in the water in the 2nd glass.
4. Wipe the measuring spoon you are using with a paper towel to get rid of the oil.
5. Try to dissolve ½ teaspoon of table salt in the water in the 3rd glass.
6. Try to dissolve ½ teaspoon of olive oil in the 4th glass.
7. Pour a little canola oil into the fifth glass.
8. Finally, try to dissolve some of the olive oil in the canola oil.

Conclusion

Say to students: If you noticed, salt and sugar blended in easily with the water. Many times we try to blend in the world. You can even discuss some ways that we try to blend in the world, such as drugs, promiscuous lifestyle, etc. However, this can be dangerous over time. If you have a diet that is high in salt or sugar, there can be a lot of complications in your life. The end result could be an increased chance of chronic diseases.

The oil that is used in the experiment represents anointing. Anointing means consecrated, set apart by God for His works and glory. In this experiment, the "anointed" liquid will not blend into the water. No matter how hard or how many times we stir the oil, it will not blend into the water. It will always rise to the top of the water. There are times when others around us will notice that we are different and that we do not blend in with the world in our actions/lifestyle. In addition, when **WE** try to go back to our old lifestyle or habits, it feels awkward and out of place.

We do see, however, that canola oil will blend with olive oil. Each of us has different anointings/gifts, but we all work together for the glory of God. 1st Cor. 12:14-26 explains the principle of spiritual gifts in detail. There are some similarities to the oils that were used in the experiment:

- All types of oil are important, but some have more recognition than others. The cost of olive oil is more expensive than vegetable oil or canola oil. However, they are both used for cooking and are very important.
- When blended together, you cannot tell the difference between the two. Unlike the mixture of salt and water, oils seem to blend in and work well with each other. The kingdom of God can use two totally different gifts and use them for the glory of God and His purpose.
- Finally, oils have different uses, but they are all critical. We all know that motor oil is not edible, but it is needed for all automobiles. Likewise lighter oils such as olive oil can not be used for machines, but they are great with pasta! Each one has a specific use, but all of them are needed.

Let us make sure that we are blending in with the right things.

Chapter 6
Through the Storm!

Summary

This is a very short lesson that could actually be combined with Chapter 5 that discusses the dangers of blending in. We know that oil was used to consecrate (or set apart) those for God's service. However, oil was also used for protection over families, temples, etc. throughout the Bible. When we are covered (or anointed) with oil, we also know that we are protected from the attacks of the devil in our lives. We literally rise above those things that would keep us from being set apart for God.

Key Background Scriptures

Matthew 5:45
Psalm 23:4
Daniel 3
Acts 16:16-34
Psalm 91:7

Say to students*:* In this experiment, we will discuss where the anointed are in the world. As Christians, we know that Jesus says that rain will fall on the just and the unjust (Matthew 5:45) and that storms will come our way. However, we can let our teens know where they stand when heavy burdens come and storms come as well.

There are three take-away points that we can learn:

1st We cannot completely avoid storms in our lives. (Matthew 5:45)

2nd God will protect us when we go through the storms. (Psalm 23)

3rd God will allow us to go through storms so that others can know that it was only God who can bring us out. (Daniel 3 and Acts 16:16-34)

Experiment 6

<u>Supplies</u>

- Nail
- Vegetable oil
- Water
- Corn syrup
- A grape
- An ice cube
- A small rock

- A tall glass

Directions

1. Take the glass and fill it about ¼ of the way with the vegetable oil
2. Add an equal amount of water to the glass
3. Add an equal amount of syrup to the glass

If you notice, there should be three layers of liquids in the glass. The syrup is at the bottom, the layer of water in the middle and finally the vegetable oil is on the top.

Say to students: You can discuss that there are a variety of individuals that go through storms, but it seems like the anointed layer (layer of oil) rose to the top of the glass...

You can also discuss that when storms do come (add rocks), they sink to the bottom with the corn syrup and yet the oil layer is not affected. You can also add ice cubes and show how they seem to stay in the layer below the oil and yet the oil layer is not affected. There is another lesson from this story as well. We must be careful as to which layer we should be in when storms come.

If we take a screw and put it in the syrup layer, then the weight of life (or the syrup in this case will keep it down) Syrup has a way of sticking to things pretty tightly. If the screw was put in the layer of water, over time the screw would become rusty because of its surroundings. The end result is that it would not be as effective as before. However, if the screw is covered in oil, (God's covering, God's promises when we read the Bible, etc.) Then the screw will work effectively. Screws and bolts work well when they are sprayed with oil, not with water or syrup.

A good closing chapter would be Psalm 91. Here is an excerpt that I found powerful….

"A thousand may fall at your side, ten thousand at your right hand, but it will not come near you."
Also…"for he will command his angels concerning to guard in your ways, they will lift you in their hands so that you will not strike your foot against a stone…"

Again, you can reiterate the fact that stones will come to hinder us, but God promises to protect us so we won't stumble.

Chapter 7

Are you full of hot air?

Summary

Have you ever watched a music awards show where winning artists have a reputation for using profanity or vulgar situations in their songs? The scenario is often the same; they approach the podium and immediately give praise to God for allowing them to win a prestigious award. Another scenario that we sometimes see is when so-called Christian politicians will make decisions based on what the constituents want to hear and not based on what would please God.

The prophet Isaiah discussed this in detail in Isaiah 1. Even though God had been faithful to the Israelites up until the time of Isaiah, the Israelites had gone astray in their behaviors and attitudes. Isaiah was sent by God to warn the Israelites of their actions as well as the consequences for those actions. He also outlined some examples for them to get back on course with God.

Key Scriptures

Exodus 18:9-12
Isaiah 1:1-5
Isaiah 1:11-14, 16-17
1st John 1:9

Say to Students

God has been so faithful- (Exodus 18:9-12)
Jethro, Moses' father-in-law, was informed by Moses on how God had delivered the Israelites from the Egyptians. In addition, he saw how God had protected them and supplied all of the Israelites' needs while they were separated from a land that they had known for hundreds of years. Jethro offered praise to God and then offered sacrifices to Him. Jethro illustrated that we should always give thanks and praise to God for who He is and what He has done.

Ask Students- **What did Isaiah say? What happened?**
Isaiah explains in Isaiah 1:1-5 that the Israelites had rebelled against God and had turned away from Him.

Say to Students….

Hot Air Principle
Yet, the Israelites continued to offer sacrifices to God as if nothing happened. God was very upset with this blowing of "hot air" to Him. God knew the Israelites' hearts and that their true allegiance was not to Him. (Isaiah 1:11-14) He also knew that their true actions spoke louder than their words to Him

God refused to hear their prayers because there was no true repentance or commitment by the Israelites to change.
Yet God outlined the things that He wanted the Israelites to stop doing. He is a compassionate Father and told them what they should do for others. He was willing to forgive. Isaiah 1:16-17.

Ask Students

What are some ways that Christians tend to have hot air and live double lives?

Example- Your friends praise God with all their might during a mid-Week Bible Study service or Sunday service. Maybe they are very active in ministry, but they are mean to others during the week, gossip, and do other ungodly things. In other words they are active in one way, but they are really blowing hot air and living a double life.

What are some ways that we can get back on track with God?

Let students explain some ways. Use Isaiah 1:17 as a guide:
- Stop doing wrong and learn to do right
- Seek justice and mercy and encourage the oppressed
- Defend the cause of the fatherless and plead the case of the widow

Let's see what happens when there is a lot of activity, but only hot air is being produced!

Experiment 7

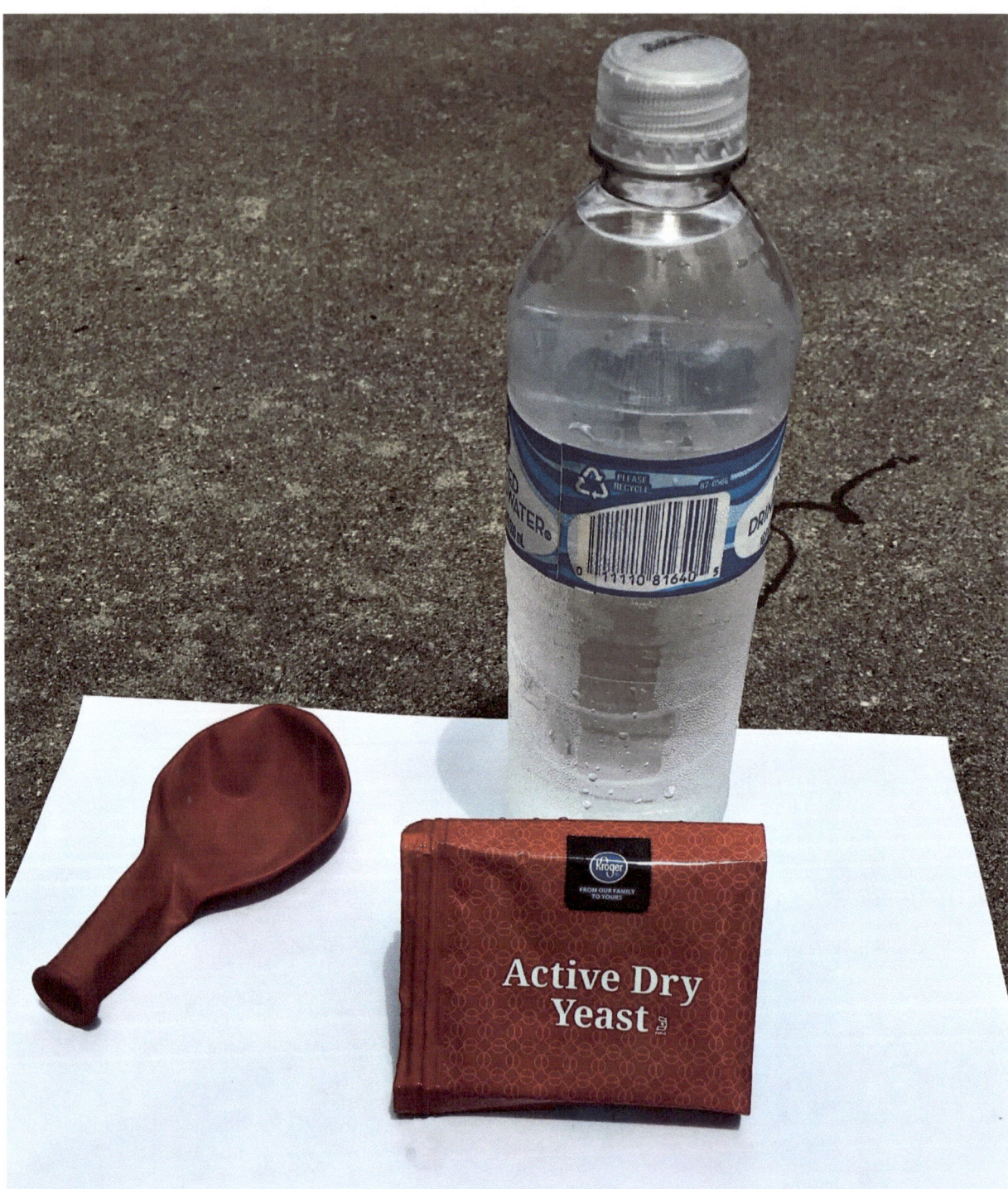

Supplies

- 1 packet of active dry yeast
- 2 tablespoons of sugar

- 1 cup of warm water
- 1 large rubber balloon
- 1 pint empty water bottle

Directions

1. Add the mixture of sugar and yeast into the cup of warm water.
2. Pour the water with the combined ingredients into the empty water bottle
3. Place the balloon over the opening of the bottle

At this point you can discuss how there is a lot of exciting activity that is going on at the bottom of the bottle. Although it is exciting, the end result is a lot of hot air (carbon dioxide that is the result of the chemical reaction) that will rise to the top. This can be seen when the balloon will eventually expand over time.

Say to students…It is a good idea to discuss the busy activity and double lives that Christians can live. On the surface it looks good, but in reality we are only producing hot air and nothing else. Our challenge today is to remain obedient to God and do right as God demands in Isaiah 1:17. If we have fallen short, God is faithful and just to forgive us of all of our sins (1st John 1:9).

Chapter 8
Spring Cleaning

Summary

During the summer, we asked our students to list a typical day for them. Many of them said that they like to sleep late, play video games and some said that they were going to summer school. Unfortunately, only a few said that they were reading the Bible on a daily basis. We highlighted several stories in the Bible that showed missionaries and evangelists who were efficacious due to their knowledge of the Scriptures.

From this knowledge, we can learn how to allow the Lord to conduct some "spring cleaning" in our lives as well as the lives of others. This experiment requires the use of old pennies and taco sauce.

Key Scriptures

Matthew 4:1-11
Acts 8:26-35
2nd Timothy 2:15
Matthew 13:18-23

Caution
Please remind your students not to rub their eyes after using the taco sauce!

Tell Students

Because Philip knew the Scriptures, he was able to interpret the book of Isaiah to the Ethiopian eunuch. In addition, Phillip was also able to share the good news of Jesus Christ. The Bible says study to show thyself approved (2nd Timothy 2:15). It is imperative that we not only know God's Word, but use wisdom to apply it to every situation that we encounter.

Temptation of Jesus
Matthew 4

Although we have discussed this passage in the past, it is very applicable here as well. Throughout this passage, the devil was persistent in every attempt to tempt Jesus. In Matthew 4:6, the devil had the audacity to quote Scripture to get his way, as well.

Despite every statement from the devil, Jesus always responded with the Word of God. Throughout our lives, many individuals will misquote or misinterpret Scripture to their advantage. It is critical that we ask God for wisdom as we learn more about the Word of God and how to apply it to our lives.

Ask Students… What happens when we don't understand the Word of God?

Say to students… The Parable of the Sower, Jesus explained the importance of the Word falling on "good soil" for hearing and understanding

Ask Students… What are the benefits of knowing the Scriptures through our daily reading?

- **Closer relationship with God**
- **Better discernment**
- **Strength in times of trouble**

Experiment 8

Supplies

- A bag of dirty pennies
- 1 jar of Taco Sauce (Mild or Medium)
- Paper Plates
- Roll of paper towels

Directions
1. Pour a tablespoon of taco sauce onto a paper plate.

2. Place a penny into the taco sauce and let it remain for approximately two minutes in the sauce.
3. After 2-5 minutes have passed, remove the pennies and you can see that the pennies are clean and shiny one side. Use the paper towels to clean hands and the pennies.

Say to students... The taco sauce represents the blood of Jesus and the pennies represent the world that needs to hear the Word of God. Despite the initial appearance of the pennies, the blood of Jesus (taco sauce) removes sins and cleans them. Even John acknowledged Jesus as "the Lamb of God, who takes away the sin of the world!" (John 1:29)

The pennies have been stained for a long time and cannot be cleaned by man alone. However, when we introduce the Word of God to a stained world, then the blood of Jesus washes away the sins and they are made new again.

I would encourage you to let each student keep the penny as a reminder of what the blood of Jesus can do. The key is to know the Scripture so others can be introduced to the blood of Jesus.

Chapter 9
The Cleaning Power of Jesus Christ

Summary

This lesson is actually a continuation of chapter 8 and the cleansing of sins. This lesson discusses the cleansing power of Jesus. You will use bleach throughout the lesson to emphasize this point. I would suggest that you use an old shirt with bleach stains to make this point effective.

Key Scriptures

Isaiah 1:18-19

Psalm 51:3-7

Romans 3:23

Caution
Please use an old shirt or piece of fabric for this experiment. Bleach can certainly ruin your outfit if you are not careful!

Say to students…
Only God can change us
Have you ever had an inconspicuous bleach stain on your favorite piece of clothing? You know you cannot get it out on your own, but yet you are willing to put up with that stain and wear your clothes anyway. In the book of Isaiah, stain represented sin. God does not want us to get comfortable with our stains and wear them anyway. He wants to remove those stains from our lives. Isaiah uses the illustration of scarlet stains. Scarlet stains were one of the hardest stains to remove during that time.

If we are truly serious and want to repent, God has the power to remove those stains from our lives so we can truly live white as snow. When discussing sin, it is amazing the things that we are not willing to remove from our lives. I took one of my favorite polo shirts to Sunday school one morning and discussed all of the good things about the shirt. I discussed that a price was paid for it, it fits well into my world (and on my body) and I like the color. Also, it is a shirt that I would feel proud to wear in public. After discussing the characteristics of the shirt, I asked the class to identify some things that were wrong with the shirt.

Some of the students noticed the bleach stains that were on the shirt. There were very small stains, but they were noticeable as students inspected the shirt. Similar to the shirt, many of us were bought with a price and we look good. However, we have some stains of sin that still remain and can be noticed as we get closer to God. We get comfortable and feel that it is okay to walk in public with those ugly stains. We expect others to accept those blemishes and move on.

From a historical perspective, crimson was used as a dye for clothing throughout the Middle East and Mediterranean regions. There were a variety of shades of red, but it was also known for its difficulty to be removed from fabric. The prophet Isaiah used crimson as an analogy to describe the "irremovable stain" of sin. Jesus has the power to remove those stains (sin) that we are comfortable with in our lives.

David acknowledged that he was born into sin and it has always been before him. He asked God to remove those sins and make him white as snow. Romans 3:23 also confirms that **all** of us have sinned and fallen short. Thank God for loving us and his desire to remove those sins from us. Sin separates us from God, but Jesus has the power to restore us and allow us to move closer to Him.

Cleaning Experiment

Supplies

- 1 clear jar (Mason jar works well)

- 1 tube of red food coloring

- 2 cups of water

- 1 cup of bleach

Directions
Say to students...
1. Pour 1 cup of water into the jar. Similar to the water in the jar, discuss how everything is transparent with God. We cannot hide our sins from God. Ask the students to name some sins (lying, gossiping, etc.)

2. For each sin, put a drop of red food coloring into the water. The red food coloring represents all of the sins that we carry as baggage. Over time, the water will become red and cloudy. In addition the view is now nontransparent through the glass.

3. Add a cup of bleach to the cup of water mixed with red food coloring. The bleach represents the cleansing power of Jesus. After waiting for several minutes, the food coloring is removed and all that remains is clear water.

God sent a Savior (Jesus) to remove those sins and help restore us into right fellowship with God. Jesus discussed the analogy of blood removing sin during the Last Supper (Matthew 26:28)

FINAL THOUGHTS

Review the fact that Jesus not only removed the sins, but He also put us into right fellowship with God again. We can actually see through the glass clearly. Things are now transparent again.

Chapter 10
Be Saturated with the Holy Spirit

Summary

There is a key to being filled with the Holy Spirit throughout the school year. As students were returning to their respective schools, we decided to discuss the saturation process. Saturation is defined as the point in which one item cannot contain another item. We will illustrate this later in this chapter.

Key Scriptures

Deuteronomy 6:6-9
Deuteronomy 20-21, 24
Deuteronomy 28

Say to students…

In Deuteronomy 6:6-9, 20-21, and verse 24, there are numerous references to the importance of keeping God's commandments. Deuteronomy 6 discusses the fact that teaching God's Word was important in all practical aspects of the Israelites' lives. The Israelites were commanded to teach their children two aspects of God:
- God expected them to love Him with all of their hearts, souls and strength
- God delivered them from Egypt and He was the only One who had provided for them.

Teaching God's Word was important in all practical aspects of the Israelites' lives. It was a total life experience, not just a Sunday ritual. Specifically in Deuteronomy 24, God tells us that we will live long and prosper. There are benefits in keeping God's blessings and the significance of them as well. Even today, there are some Jews who still put Scriptures into small boxes and bind them on their foreheads. This is to symbolize the importance of keeping God's Word close to their hearts.

Finally, Deuteronomy 28 discusses the benefits of keeping God's commandments and also the consequences of not keeping God's commandments.

Saturation Experiment

Materials Needed:
2 cups of water
4-5 tablespoons of salt

Directions

1. Use a large glass or bowl and pour in cups of water.

Say to students…

2. Pour in 1 tablespoon of salt and begin to stir. Discuss the fact that this 1 tablespoon of salt represents a Christian that only goes to church once a week, but they are not very effective throughout the week. Their "salt" can be easily be diluted with something else.

3. Add another tablespoon of salt and continue to stir. This represents a Christian who not only goes to church on the weekends, but they are now involved in a Bible study during the week. However, they don't read their Bible daily and still live a lifestyle that is opposite to other Christians.

4. Finally, put the remaining tablespoons of salt into the bowl and continue to stir. If you notice, the extra salt will begin to fall to the bottom. This is called the point of saturation, a point where the liquid (water) can no longer hold any of the substance (salt). At this point, we discussed that we are so filled with God's commandments, the Holy Spirit and his blessings, that we now "spill" this on to others.

As students returned to school for the fall, we challenged them to become filled with the Holy Spirit and allow themselves to become saturated with Him.

Chapter 11

Other Sunday School Lessons for Different Occasions

Summary

Even though these lessons do not have a science experiment, we found them to be very effective.

Goals vs. Stretch Goals

This lesson is great for pre-teens at the close of an academic year. As we get to the end of the school year, we focused on one academic goal and one stretch goal for the upcoming year.

Key Scriptures

Philippians 4:13
Jeremiah 29:11
1st Samuel 9: 15-17, 21
1st Samuel 10: 6, 20-22
Judges 6:1-16

Say to students…

Today, we are going to focus on two individuals who saw themselves differently; Saul and Gideon. God has big plans for us and the Word of God says that we can do all things through Christ who strengthens us.(Philippians 4:13) God's Word also says He knows the plans that He has for us, plans to give us a hope and a future. (Jeremiah 29:11)

Portrait of Saul-

1st Samuel 9: 15-17. God had plans for Saul to lead His people against the Philistines. The Israelites wanted a king and God heard their prayers. Saul was unaware of the calling, but God had already ordained it.

1st Samuel 9:21- Saul rejected his calling, but Samuel the prophet continued to treat him as royalty.

1st Samuel 10:6 When God has plans for you, He will equip you to do the work.

1st Samuel 10: 20-22 Saul was found **amongst** the baggage. He was still willing to assume the position of leadership. How many times have you been asked to do something and not taken advantage of the opportunity?

REMEMBER, WHERE YOU WILL BE FIVE YEARS FROM NOW IS A FUNCTION OF THE CONNECTIONS YOU MAKE WITH OTHERS
When you don't follow God's directions or seek Godly counsel, you will fail.

1st Samuel 15: 1-3 God's instructions were given.

1st Samuel 15: 7-9- Saul took matters into his own hands. Samuel told him, "It's better to obey God than give sacrifices." At that moment, Saul was rejected by God to lead Israel.

After Saul was rejected, David was anointed to be the next king. Saul became very jealous and insecure of David (1st Samuel 18: 10-11). David was almost killed by Saul.

1st Samuel 28: 3, 7 16-19. Saul went back on his word and consulted a witch rather than God. In the end, he lost everything.

God has big plans for all of us, but if we don't assume the responsibility or set good goals, we will fail in the end.

Portrait of Gideon

Have students read Judges 6:1-10 aloud.

Ask students...
What is the comparison to some dark things today?

God calls Gideon vs. 10-16
Ask students...
Vs. 12- Who does God say that Gideon is? (mighty man of valor)
Vs. 15- Who did Gideon say he was?
Vs. 16 What did God do with Gideon?

Mother's Day Lesson

Key Scriptures

Genesis 16:11-15
Genesis 27:1-24, 30, 41
1st Samuel 1:10-11, 27-28
Luke 1:26-38

Summary
The learning objective is for students to distinguish mothers who honored God and those who didn't honor God.   Women such as Sarai, Rebekah, Hannah and Mary are highlighted. The Spiritual lesson is that we should trust God in all situations and that we should never doubt Him.

Say to students...
We need to trust God in all situations.   In Proverbs 3:5, the Bible says to "Trust in the Lord with all your heart, and lean not on your own understanding; in all your ways acknowledge him and he will make your paths straight." Unfortunately, some of the women did not trust God and the end results were devastating.

THE LESSON:

As we focus on Mother's Day, we want to focus on some women who honored God in their relationships and those who didn't honor God.

Mothers who didn't honor God

Sarai

Sarai tried to take over God's job of being the One who blesses us and shows us favor. She became impatient and decided to run things her way. Rather than waiting on God, Sarai took matters in her own hand. The end result was that Hagar (Sarai's servant) had a son instead. Although God protected Hagar, He also indicated that Ishmael (Hagar's son) will be against everyone and will live in hostility toward all of his brothers.

Rebekah

Like Sarai, Rebekah was impatient with God and decided to take matters into her own hands, as well. God had promised great things to Jacob already. With Rebekah's help, though, Jacob tricked his father (Isaac) into giving him the blessing.

The end result was that Esau left angry and hurt without the blessings of his father. In addition, Esau was determined to kill Jacob. Although Jacob was blessed, he literally ran from his family and especially Esau.

Mothers who did honor God

Hannah

Hannah was barren and unable to have children, as well. Her husband interceded on her behalf and she eventually was able to have children. She made a promise to dedicate her firstborn God (Samuel) back to God. He eventually moved to the temple and became a great prophet for God.

Mary, Mother of Jesus

Despite the reputation of being an unwed mother pledged to Joseph, Mary knew that she had found favor with God. She trusted the words of God through the angel Gabriel and was determined to trust God throughout the process. Ultimately, Jesus became the Savior of the world and died for our sins.

www.ingramcontent.com/pod-product-compliance
Lightning Source LLC
Chambersburg PA
CBHW060759090426

42736CB00002B/83